Alejandro de Artep
Sex After Your 25ᵗʰ Anniversary

ISBN-13: 978-1508898870
ISBN-10: 1508898871

DISCLAIMER

TBB2HFC or **The Blank Books 2 Have Fun Collection** is intended as a fun gift to make your friends and loved ones smile. Neither the author nor the publisher assume any responsibility for any errors or omissions, nor do they represent or warrant that the information, ideas, plans, actions, suggestions, or methods of operation contained herein are in all cases true, accurate, appropriate, or legal. It is the reader's responsibility to consult with his or her own advisor or an expert in a specific area before putting any of the enclosed information, plans, examples, ideas, or practices into play. The author and the publisher specifically disclaim any liability resulting from the use of application of the information contained in this book. The information and ideas are not intended to serve as legal advice related to individual situations. All of the research in the book is based on the author's experiences and opinions. The author's model of the world, his values, beliefs and thinking processes represent important limitations, which should be taken into account when reading the book. Further study, skills and competences, and an expert opinion, should be taken into consideration before any action is taken.

For more information about translation rights, please contact us at thecreativepublishers@gmail.com.

Sex After Your 25th Anniversary

Alejandro de Artep

In the following pages there is a detailed description of all the sex you are going to have after your 25th anniversary.
Enjoy the reading. ☺

(This page is intentionally left blank)

(This page is intentionally left blank)

(This page is intentionally left blank)

(This page is intentionally left blank)

(This page is intentionally left blank)

(This page is intentionally left blank)

(This page is intentionally left blank)

(This page is intentionally left blank)

(This page is intentionally left blank)

(This page is intentionally left blank)

(This page is intentionally left blank)

(This page is intentionally left blank)

(This page is intentionally left blank)

(This page is intentionally left blank)

(This page is intentionally left blank)

(This page is intentionally left blank)

(This page is intentionally left blank)

(This page is intentionally left blank)

(This page is intentionally left blank)

(This page is intentionally left blank)

(This page is intentionally left blank)

(This page is intentionally left blank)

(This page is intentionally left blank)

(This page is intentionally left blank)

(This page is intentionally left blank)

(This page is intentionally left blank)

(This page is intentionally left blank)

(This page is intentionally left blank)

(This page is intentionally left blank)

(This page is intentionally left blank)

(This page is intentionally left blank)

(This page is intentionally left blank)

(This page is intentionally left blank)

(This page is intentionally left blank)

(This page is intentionally left blank)

(This page is intentionally left blank)

(This page is intentionally left blank)

(This page is intentionally left blank)

(This page is intentionally left blank)

(This page is intentionally left blank)

(This page is intentionally left blank)

(This page is intentionally left blank)

(This page is intentionally left blank)

(This page is intentionally left blank)

(This page is intentionally left blank)

(This page is intentionally left blank)

(This page is intentionally left blank)

(This page is intentionally left blank)

(This page is intentionally left blank)

(This page is intentionally left blank)

(This page is intentionally left blank)

(This page is intentionally left blank)

(This page is intentionally left blank)

(This page is intentionally left blank)

(This page is intentionally left blank)

(This page is intentionally left blank)

(This page is intentionally left blank)

(This page is intentionally left blank)

(This page is intentionally left blank)

(This page is intentionally left blank)

(This page is intentionally left blank)

(This page is intentionally left blank)

(This page is intentionally left blank)

(This page is intentionally left blank)

(This page is intentionally left blank)

(This page is intentionally left blank)

(This page is intentionally left blank)

(This page is intentionally left blank)

(This page is intentionally left blank)

(This page is intentionally left blank)

(This page is intentionally left blank)

(This page is intentionally left blank)

(This page is intentionally left blank)

(This page is intentionally left blank)

(This page is intentionally left blank)

I scared you a little bit, didn't I?
Just kidding – the real sex is yet to begin. ☺

After the 25ᵗʰ anniversary sex becomes much, much better, they say. The secret is to practice a lot. So practice, practice, practice. ☺ Remember to love each other a little bit more every day.

BE HAPPY AND ENJOY EVERY MOMENT OF YOUR RELATIONSHIP.

Made in the USA
Middletown, DE
26 October 2016